THE GRACE DEVOTIONAL
FIFTY-TWO HAPPY WEEKS WITH GOD

CHARLES MWEWA

Copyright © 2021 Charles Mwewa

PUBLISHED BY:

ACP, Ottawa

Canada

All rights reserved.

ISBN: 978-1-988251-51-6

DEDICATION

This book is solemnly dedicated to the worship of God the Father, the Son, and the Holy Spirit in the spirit of purity and reverence, and in the context of pure religion. The glory of our God and the magnificence of His Church transcend any form of human adulation or objective.

CONTENTS

ABOUT THIS BOOK i
    Purpose i
    Usage i
    Textual Readings ii
    Power of Confession iii
1 LET US PASS OVER 1
    Text: Mark 4:35-41 1
    Today's Confession 2
    Intercession 2
    Prayer Power 2
2 FATHER, FORGIVE THEM 3
    Text: Luke 23:34 3
    Today's Confession 3
    Intercession 4
    Prayer Power 4
3 BEHOLD, I MAKE ALL THINGS NEW 5
    Text: Revelation 21: 1-5 5
    Today's Confession 6
    Intercession 6

- Prayer Power 6

4 JUDGE NOT 7
- Text: Matt. 7:1-5 7
- Today's Confession 7
- Intercession 8
- Prayer Power 8

5 LOST BUT FOUND 9
- Text: Luke 15:11-24 9
- Today's Confession 10
- Intercession 11
- Prayer Power 12

6 A MIND MADE UP 13
- Text: Romans 12: 1-2 13
- Today's Confession 13
- Intercession 14
- Prayer Power 14

7 MALE AND FEMALE 15
- Text: Matthew 19:4-6 15
- Today's Confession 15
- Intercession 16
- Prayer Power 16

8 REPAY NO EVIL FOR EVIL 17
- Text: Romans 12:17-19 17
- Today's Confession 17
- Intercession 18
- Prayer Power 18

9 WHERE MY HELP COMES 19
Text: Psalm 121:1,2,7 and 8 19
Today's Confession 19
Intercession 20
Prayer Power 20

10 CALLED ACCORDING TO HIS PURPOSE 21
Text: Romans 8: 28-29 21
Today's Confession 21
Intercession 22
Prayer Power 22

11 LEAVING TO CLEAVE 23
Text: Mark 10: 1-12 23
Today's Confession 24
Intercession 24
Prayer Power 24

12 HELP MY UNBELIEF, LORD 25
Text: Mark 9: 23 and 24 25
Today's Confession 25
Intercession 26
Prayer Power 26

13 BE FILLED 27
Text: 1 Thess. 5: 18-20 27
Today's Confession 27
Intercession 28
Prayer Power 28

14 CHILDREN OF FREEDOM 29

- Text: John 8: 34-36 29
- Today's Confession 29
- Intercession 30
- Prayer Power 30

15 DESIRE NO VAINGLORY 31
- Text: Galatians 5:26 31
- Today's Confession 31
- Intercession 32
- Prayer Power 32

16 PERISH NOT 33
- Text: John 3:16 33
- Today's Confession 33
- Intercession 34
- Prayer Power 34

17 NEGLECT NOT YOUR PROFESSION 35
- Text: Hebrews 4: 14-16 35
- Today's Confession 35
- Intercession 36
- Prayer Power 36

18 NO, NOT IN ISRAEL 37
- Text: Matthew 8:5-11 37
- Today's Confession 37
- Intercession 38
- Prayer Power 38

19 TO SEEK AND TO SAVE 39
- Text: Luke 19:10 39

    Today's Confession 39

    Intercession 40

    Prayer Power 40

20 I CAN DO ALL THINGS 41

    Text: Phil. 4: 12 and 13 41

    Today's Confession 41

    Intercession 42

    Prayer Power 42

21 SEVEN TIMES IN A DAY 43

    Text: Luke 17: 3 and 4 43

    Today's Confession 43

    Intercession 44

    Prayer Power 44

22 THE PRAYER OF FAITH 45

    Text: James 5: 14-16 45

    Today's Confession 45

    Intercession 46

    Prayer Power 46

23 WHAT MANNER OF A MAN IS THIS? 47

    Text: Mark 4:37-41 47

    Today's Confession 47

    Intercession 48

    Prayer Power 48

24 AN EXAMPLE TO FOLLOW 49

    Text: 1 Peter 2: 20-23 49

    Today's Confession 49

Intercession 50

Prayer Power 50

25 SAVE US FROM LIES 51

Text: John 8:44 51

Today's Confession 51

Intercession 52

Prayer Power 52

26 SUP WITH ME 53

Text: Revelation 3: 20 53

Today's Confession 53

Intercession 54

Prayer Power 54

27 AS UNTO THE LORD 55

Text: Colossians 3: 17, 23 55

Today's Confession 55

Intercession 56

Prayer Power 56

28 CALMER OF HEARTS 57

Text: John 14: 27 57

Today's Confession 57

Intercession 58

Prayer Power 58

29 WHEN I PRAY 59

Text: Luke 11:1 59

Today's Confession 59

Intercession 61

- Prayer Power 62

30 AGAINST SUCH THERE IS NO LAW 63
- Text: Galatians 5:19-23 63
- Today's Confession 63
- Intercession 64
- Prayer Power 64

31 I WILL INSTRUCT YOU 65
- Text: Psalm 32:8 65
- Today's Confession 65
- Intercession 66
- Prayer Power 66

32 A LIGHT BURDEN 67
- Text: Mathew 11:28 67
- Today's Confession 67
- Intercession 68
- Prayer Power 68

33 LOVE WORKS 69
- Text: Romans 13:10 69
- Today's Confession 69
- Intercession 70
- Prayer Power 70

34 KNOW YOU NOT 71
- Text: 1 Corinthians 3: 16 and 17 71
- Today's Confession 71
- Intercession 72
- Prayer Power 72

35 TRIUMPHANT IN CHRIST 73
Text: 2 Corinthians 2:14 73
Today's Confession 73
Intercession 74
Prayer Point 74

36 I HAVE LEARNED CONTENTMENT 75
Text: Phil. 4:11 75
Today's Confession 75
Intercession 76
Prayer Power 76

37 BLESS THOSE WHO CURSE YOU 77
Text: Luke 6:27-28 77
Today's Confession 77
Intercession 78
Prayer Point 78

38 BELIEVE…AND…RECEIVED 79
Text: John 1:12 79
Today's Confession 79
Intercession 80
Prayer Power 80

39 WITNESSES TO PEOPLE 81
Text: Acts 1:8 81
Today's Confession 81
Intercession 82
Prayer Power 82

40 HE MUST INCREASE 83

- Text: John 3:30-31 83
- Today's Confession 83
- Intercession 84
- Prayer Power 84

41 GOD EXPANDS HIS PEOPLE 85
- Text: 1 Corinthians 3: 6-7 85
- Today's Confession 85
- Intercession 86
- Prayer Power 86

42 IN MY FATHER'S BUSINESS 87
- Text: Luke 2:49-52 87
- Today's Confession 87
- Intercession 88
- Prayer Power 88

43 THE WORD OF GOD GREW 89
- Text: Acts 6:7 89
- Today's Confession 89
- Intercession 90
- Prayer Power 90

44 JESUS IS PRECIOUS 91
- Text: 1 Peter 2:1-7 91
- Today's Confession 91
- Intercession 92
- Prayer Power 92

45 I WILL MULTIPLY YOU 93
- Text: Hebrews 6: 13-15 93

- Today's Confession 93
- Intercession 94
- Prayer Power 94

46 AT YOUR WORD 95
- Text: Luke 5:4-5 95
- Today's Confession 95
- Intercession 96
- Prayer Power 96

47 ADD TO FAITH… 97
- Text: 2 Peter 1:5-7 97
- Today's Confession 97
- Intercession 98
- Prayer Point 98

48 SINGLENESS OF HEART 99
- Text: Acts 2:46-47 99
- Today's Confession 99
- Intercession 100
- Prayer Power 100

49 AN EXCELLENT SPIRIT 101
- Text: Daniel 6:3 101
- Today's Confession 101
- Intercession 102
- Prayer Point 102

50 THE SUPERIORITY OF WISDOM 103
- Text: 1 Kings 4:30-34 103
- Today's Confession 103

  Intercession 104
  Prayer Power 104
51 SWEET INFLUENCES 105
  Text: Job 38:31 105
  Today's Confession 105
  Intercession 106
  Prayer Power 106
52 ALL OF GRACE 107
  Text: John 1:14 107
  Today's Confession 107
  Intercession 108
  Prayer Power 108
ABOUT THE AUTHOR 109
AUTHOR'S CONTACT 110
INDEX 111

ACKNOWLEDGMENTS

My cherished memories go to Sister Irene Dubelt who assisted with copy editing and provided useful insights in the initial stages. Grace and peace be hers through the blessed name of our Lord and Savior, Jesus Christ.

ABOUT THIS BOOK

Purpose

This book is to be used primarily for the purposes of devotion by any Church or individual who believes in the power of prayer. It is compiled as a litany for conducting group or personal worship services or exercises for prayers and invocations. It can also be used as an aid in private devotion and prayers. Its secret is in the reading of the confessions deliberately selected to equip the soul and inspire the spirit. People have wondered why they pray and don't see results. The answer is partly due to negligence in confessing the portions of the Bible relevant to their situation. This book is Bible-focused; nothing in this book is man-premeditated. From the theme (text) to prayer power, everything is Bible-based. The consistent use of this book will result in inspired and empowered individuals and in an equipped Church.

Usage

This book comprises fifty-two chapters (one whole year) of confessions and intercessions. It is designed to be used as litany for conducting services in private and public devotion. It consists of a text, today's confession, intercessions and prayer power. The chapter topic is the thesis governing the general worship for the week in number; the text is the passage from the Bible on which the theme is based; today's confession is a series of invocations and decrees taken from a combination of scriptural verses in the Bible; intercessions are a solemn petitions for various needs for the week in number; and the prayer power marks the petitioner's invitation to pray for the suggested request(s).

Textual Readings

Reading the Word of God aloud is an integral part of a biblical worship service. A good example of this is illustrated in the book of Nehemiah:

> And Ezra the priest brought the law before the congregation both of men and women, and all that could hear with understanding, upon the first day of the seventh month. And he read therein before the street that was before the water gate from the morning until midday, before the men and the women, and those that could understand; and the ears of all the people were attentive unto the book of the law. And Ezra the scribe stood upon a pulpit of wood, which they had made for the purpose.... And Ezra opened the book in the sight of all the people; (for he was above all the people); and when he opened it, all the people stood up: And Ezra blessed the LORD, the great God. And all the people answered, Amen, Amen, with lifting up their hands: and they bowed their heads and worshiped the LORD with their faces to the ground.[1]

Ezra read the book of the law publicly before the congregation of the children of Israel. This was a type of the Church congregation. The New Testament Church is called

---

[1] Nehemiah. 8:2-6

to the reading of the Word of God aloud for the congregation to hear, too. From the passage above, seven principles have been identified as governing the public reading of the Bible:

- It must be read before the whole congregation;

- The congregation must both hear it and understand it;

- The congregation must pay attention to the details of the reading;

- The leader in the reading of the Word of God must be above everyone else; he or she must stand elevated before a pulpit so that everyone can see him or her;

- The congregation must stand up when the Bible is being read publicly;

- The congregation must respond with an "Amen" as a form of agreement after the Word of God has been read;

- And doing this is a form of public worship and must be encouraged in the Church.

Power of Confession

Confession is the end result of our faith, just like Apostle Paul says, "We having the same spirit of faith, according as it is written, I believed, and therefore have I spoken [confessed]; we also believe, and therefore speak [confess]."[2]

What we believe in is meaningless until we confess it. Confession creates what we believe and sets it in motion. This devotion book (Guide) gives the Church and individuals an occasion to publicly confess the Word of God week by week throughout an entire year for a continuously *happy* relationship with God.

During today's confession, the entire congregation may rise, just like when the text is being read, and together make the confession. In case of individual confession, there may not be a need for standing up and confessing loudly; a quiet, closet-attitude may be preferred.[3] After this is done, faith will grow, the Church will be edified and individual believers will be revived.

> In you I put my trust,
> When shall I come and appear before you
> Oh, God, my Lord?
> My heart longs, and even faints for you,
> My Blessed Lord.

---

[2] 2 Corinthians 4:13
[3] See Matthew 6:6 [But when you pray, go into your room, close the door and pray to your Father, who is unseen. Then your Father, who sees what is done in secret, will reward you – NIV]

1 LET US PASS OVER

Text: Mark 4:35-41

"And the same day, when the even was come, he saith unto them, let us pass over unto the other side. And when they had sent away the multitude, they took him even as he was in the ship. And there were also with him other little ships. And there arose a great storm of wind, and the waves beat into the ship, so that it was now full. And he was in the hinder part of the ship, asleep on a pillow: and they awake him, and say unto him, Master, cares thou not that we perish? And he arose, and rebuked the wind and said unto the sea, peace, be still. And the wind ceased, and there was a great calm. And he said unto them, why are ye so fearful? How is it that ye have no faith? And they feared exceedingly, and said one to another, what manner of man is this that even the wind and the sea obey him?"

Today's Confession

When I am afraid, Lord, I will trust in you. In God my fortress I will put my faith. I will not fear because my trust is in God. I will not fear what flesh and blood can do to me. In Jesus' name…

Intercession

Today, we remember all those who are under the bandage of fear. We pray that they will soon realize the enormous power found in the name of Jesus. We ask specifically that, Lord, you will deliver them from the hand of Satan and bring them into your glorious light. Let their fear be turned into faith. All these we ask in Jesus' name, Amen!

Prayer Power

Releasing uncommon blessings for victorious living…

2 FATHER, FORGIVE THEM

Text: Luke 23:34

> " Then said Jesus, Father, forgive them; for they know not what they do. And they parted his raiment and cast lots."

Today's Confession

Plead my cause, Lord, with those who strive with me and fight against they who fight against me. Take hold of your weapons and stand up for my help. Save me O Lord by your name. Indeed, my enemies have risen up against me and my oppressors seek after my soul. But you are my helper and the one who upholds my soul. A thousand shall fall at my side and ten thousands at my right hand, but they shall not come near me. Only with my eyes shall I behold the destruction of my enemies. Because I have made the LORD my refuge and habitation, there shall no evil befall me and no calamity shall come near me. The LORD has given his angels charge over me, to keep me in my entire ways. In Jesus' name…

Intercession

Today, we remember all those who are under the bandage of Satan and other forms of enemy attack. We pray that they will soon realize the tremendous victory they already have in the blood of Jesus. We ask specifically that, Lord, you will deliver them from the hand of Satan and bring them into your glorious light. Let this attack be turned into victory. All these we ask in Jesus' name, Amen!

Prayer Power

Breaking impossible situations with extraordinary faith…in Jesus' name!

3 BEHOLD, I MAKE ALL THINGS NEW

Text: Revelation 21: 1-5

"And I saw a new heaven and a new earth: For the first heaven and the first earth were passed away; and there was no more sea. And I John saw the holy city, New Jerusalem, coming down from God out of heaven, prepared as a bride adorned for her husband. And I heard a great voice out of heaven saying, behold, the tabernacle of God is with men [and women], and he will dwell with them, and they shall be his people, and God himself shall be with them, and be their God. And God shall wipe away all tears from their eyes; and there shall be no more death, sorrow nor crying, neither shall there be any more pain for the former things are passed away. And he that sat upon the throne said, behold, I make all things new. And he said unto me, write; for these words are true and faithful."

Today's Confession

Lord, you are the one who heals the broken-hearted and binds up their wounds. I am not ignorant of your purposes and plan towards me, and therefore, I will not be in sorrow. My hope is in you, dear Lord, and I believe that Jesus died and rose again. When you come back in your glory, Lord, you shall descent from heaven with a shout of an archangel and with a trumpet of God, and the dead in Christ shall rise. And together with us who shall be alive, we will meet you in the clouds and thereby be with you forever. With this in mind, I am comforted. In Jesus' name…

Intercession

Today, we remember all those who are under sorrow and a state of heart brokenness by virtue of the loss of a loved one or a misfortune. We pray that they will soon realize the tremendous comfort already available in the Holy Spirit. We ask specifically that, Lord, you will wipe away their tears and turn their grieving into dancing. All these we ask in Jesus' name, Amen!

Prayer Power

Bring the rains of revival, O God…Wipe out pandemics, including Covid, from our midst….

4 JUDGE NOT

Text: Matt. 7:1-5

"Judge not, that ye be not judged. For with what judgment ye judge, ye shall be judged and with what measure ye mete, it shall be measured to you again. And why beholdest thou the mote that is in thy brother's eye, but considerest not the beam that is in thine own eye? Or how wilt thou say to thy brother let me pull out the mote out of thine eye; and, behold, a beam is in thine own eye? Thou hypocrite, first cast out the beam out of thine own eye; and then shalt thou see clearly to cast out the mote out of thy brother's eye."

Today's Confession

I will not judge my brother or sister, for we shall all stand before the judgment seat of Christ. It is written that the Lord lives and every knee shall bow and every tongue shall confess that Jesus Christ is Lord. I am also aware that I shall give account of myself to God. I will, therefore, not judge anyone and I will not place a stumbling block against my brother or sister. Lord, I acknowledge that you shall bring to light the hidden things of darkness and make manifest all the counsels of the hearts. Lord, even though I am grieved in my heart, I will still praise you. Sometimes I am unwise and ignorant. Nevertheless, you are always with me and you will hold me by your right hand. You will guide me by your wise counsel and afterward receive me in glory. Lord, there is joy in my heart, because I have no one in heaven but you, and there is nothing upon the earth I desire besides you. In Jesus' name…

Intercession

Today, we remember all those who are under the judgment of men and of the law. We pray that they will soon realize that even in their direst hour you are there with them. We ask specifically that, Lord, you will shield them from all appearances of injustice and deliver them from men's criticism. For others we ask that you save them from the pending imprisonment. We ask for all these in Jesus' name, Amen!

Prayer Power

Thank God we are free…and slaves to no one…

5 LOST BUT FOUND

Text: Luke 15:11-24

"And he said a certain man had two sons: And the younger of them said to his father, father, give me the portion of goods that falleth to me. And he divided unto them his living. And not many days after the younger son gathered all together, and took his journey into a far country, and there wasted his substance with riotous living. And when he had spent all, there arose a mighty famine in that land; and he began to be in want. And he went and joined himself to a citizen of that country; and he sent him into his fields to feed swine [pigs]. And he would fain have filled his belly with the husks that the swine did eat and no man gave unto him. And when he came to himself, he said, how many hired servants of my father's have bread enough and to spare, and I perish with hunger! I will arise and go to my father, and will say unto him, father, I have sinned against heaven, and before thee, and am no more worthy to be called thy son: make me as one of thy hired servants. And he arose and came to his father. But when he was yet a great way off, his father saw him, and had compassion, and ran, and fell on his neck, and kissed him. And the son said unto him, father, I have sinned against heaven, and in thy sight, and am no more worthy to be called thy son. But the father said to his servants, bring forth the best robe, and put it on him; and put a ring on his hand, and shoes on his feet: And bring hither the fatted calf, and kill it; and let us eat, and be merry: For this my son was dead, and is alive again; he was lost, and is found. And they began to be merry."

Today's Confession

Heavenly Father, you are light and in you there is no darkness. If I say that I have fellowship with you, and still walk in darkness, I lie, and do not have the truth. But if I walk in the light as you are in the light, I have fellowship with you and with fellow believers, and the blood of your Son, my Lord Jesus Christ, cleanses me from all sin. If I say that I have no sin, I deceive myself, and the truth is not in me.

LORD, I am confessing my sins to you because you are faithful and just to forgive and clean me from all unrighteousness. I thank you, Father, because as far as the east is from the west, so far you have removed my transgressions from me.

I plead with you to have mercy upon me, O God, according to your loving kindness. Wash me from my hidden faults and sin, for I acknowledge my transgression and my sin is ever before me. Against you only have I sinned and done evil in your sight. In this you are justified when you speak and you are holy when you judge. In iniquity I was shaped; and in sin did my mother conceive me. God, you desire truth in my inward parts, and in the hidden parts you make me to know wisdom.

Wash me and I shall be clean and make me to hear joy

and gladness; that the bones, which you have broken, may be strong again. Also create a clean heart in me, O God, and renew a right spirit within me. Do not cast me away from your presence, and do not take your Holy Spirit from me. Restore to me the joy of my salvation and uphold me with your free Spirit. In Jesus' name…

Intercession

Today, we remember all those who are under a heavy burden of sin. We pray that they will soon realize that they already have forgiveness through the blood of Jesus. No matter what they have done, Lord. No matter how big or small their faults. If they have sinned against you inadvertently, forgive. If they have sinned against you wilfully, even that forgive. If they have tested the goodness of the Lord before and now they have slidden back, forgive and restore. If they have doubted you, ignored you, or poked fingers at you, please forgive. If they have fought against your will, rebelled against your love and kindness, forgive. If they have mocked and shown contempt to you, even that do forgive. If they think that they have done nothing wrong, Holy Spirit convict them of sin. If they are too proud to confess their offences to you, Holy God, do forgive. We ask specifically that, Father Lord, you will clean them from every sin and transgression and restore them to a right standing with you. All these we ask in Jesus' name, Amen!

Prayer Power

There shall be no premature death among us....

6 A MIND MADE UP

Text: Romans 12: 1-2

" I beseech you therefore, brethren, by the mercies of God, that ye present your bodies a living sacrifice, holy, acceptable unto God, which is your reasonable service. And be not conformed to this world: but be ye transformed by the renewing of your mind, that ye may prove what is that good, and acceptable, and perfect, will of God."

Today's Confession

I seek for godly wisdom, that which is pure, peaceable, gentle, reasonable and full of mercy. May I be a tree that bears good fruits, unwavering and without hypocrisy. May I also be a single-minded person that I may be stable in all my ways! By the mercies of God, may I be a living sacrifice, holy and acceptable unto God. May I not be conformed to the pattern of this selfish world, rather, be renewed in my mind and soul that I may do all the perfect will of God. In Jesus' name…

Intercession

Today, we remember all those who are under the bondage of mental and spiritual strongholds. We pray that they will soon realize that there is freedom in the death of Christ. We ask specifically that, Lord, you will open their minds to find liberty and peace that passes all understanding. All these we ask in Jesus' name, Amen!

Prayer Power

No one that believes in Jesus shall be put to shame…

7 MALE AND FEMALE

Text: Matthew 19:4-6

"And he answered and said unto them, have ye not read, that he which made them at the beginning made them male and female, and said, for this cause shall a man leave father and mother, and shall cleave to his wife: and they twain shall be one flesh. Wherefore they are no more twain, but one flesh. What therefore God hath joined together, let not man put asunder."

Today's Confession

I submit myself to my partner as unto the Lord, not due to human humiliation but in the fear of God. There is order in godly relationships so that the husband is the head of the wife, and the wife is a wise helper. This is right because Christ himself is the head of the Church, and he is the Savior of the body. I will also honor marriage and respect the marriage vows because marriage itself is honorable in all and the nuptial bed undefiled. I understand also that whole mongers and adulterers will be judged. For this reason, I exonerate [clear] myself of any wanton thoughts and lusts and surrender my relationships to God for sanctification. In Jesus' name…

Intercession

Today, we remember all those who are under the covenant of holy matrimony. We pray that they will soon realize that it is God who first instituted the sanctity of marriage and blessed it for the goodness of the family. We ask specifically that, Lord, you will also remember those who have lost direction in marriage and those still seeking for a life mate that you will answer their prayers speedily. All these we ask in Jesus' name, Amen!

Prayer Power

Remember me, and the work of love that I do in your name, Lord my God…

8 REPAY NO EVIL FOR EVIL

Text: Romans 12:17-19

"Recompense to no man evil for evil. Provide things honest in the sight of all men. If it were possible, as much as it lieth in you, live peaceably with all men. Dearly beloved, avenge not yourselves, but rather give place unto wrath: for it is written, vengeance is mine; I will repay, saith the Lord."

Today's Confession

I want to be careful to see that I do not render evil for evil to any person. My desire is to follow that which is good, both to myself and to others. To this I was called, because Christ also suffered for me, leaving me an example, that I should follow his steps. Christ did not sin, and neither was guile found in his mouth: when he was reviled, he reviled not again. When he suffered, he did not threaten, but committed himself to him that judges righteously. Help me today not to revenge against those that wrong me. In Jesus' name…

Intercession

Today, we remember all those who have been offended and can't find strength to release. We pray that through the power of the Holy Spirit they will be enabled to forgive. We ask specifically that, Lord, you will also remember those who have themselves offended others that they will soon realize how unhealthy it is to their own soul. All these we ask in Jesus' name, Amen!

Prayer Power

Forgive all and forget, lest your own prayers be hindered…

9 WHERE MY HELP COMES

Text: Psalm 121:1,2,7 and 8

"I will lift up mine eyes unto the hills, from whence cometh my help. My help comes from the LORD, which made heaven and earth. The LORD shall preserve thee from all evil: he shall preserve thy soul. The LORD shall preserve thy going out and thy coming in from this time forth, and even forevermore."

Today's Confession

As for me I will call upon God and he shall save me. Evening, morning and afternoon I will not cease to pray and cry to my God, and he shall answer me. From the end of the earth I will cry to God even when my heart is overwhelmed. Oh, Lord, lead me to the rock that is higher than I! You have been a shelter to me, and a strong tower from my enemies. When my feet slipped, your mercies, Oh, God, held me. You comfort my soul in the multitudes of my thoughts. Lord, you are my help in terrible and trying times. My soul trusts in you, and from you comes my salvation. In Jesus' name…

Intercession

Today, we remember all those who are overwhelmed by their own insecurities and pride. We pray that they will soon realize that Christ's yoke is easy and his burden is light. We ask specifically that, Lord, you will help them out and bring a lesson of humility to their attention. All these we ask in Jesus' name, Amen!

Prayer Power

Breaking the spirit of pride and arrogance in Jesus' name…

10 CALLED ACCORDING TO HIS PURPOSE

Text: Romans 8: 28-29

" And we know that all things work together for good to them that love God, to them who are the called according to his purpose. For whom he did foreknow, he also did predestinate to be conformed to the image of his Son, that he might be the firstborn among many brethren."

Today's Confession

Many times I am troubled, yet not distressed; I am perplexed, but not in despair. Sometimes I am persecuted, but never forsaken; I am cast down, but by no means destroyed! My faith is growing stronger with every passing challenge because I know that when I am afflicted it is but for a short time. And this works for me far more exceedingly. I don't look at things that are seen, but at the things that are not seen and are eternal. When I am oppressed, the Lord is my refuge. I will offer thanksgiving and call upon God in my times of trouble. Even though things currently seem hard, I am assured they will turn out for my good. In Jesus' name…

Intercession

Today, we remember all those Christians who are beginning to doubt their faith in God because of what they are going through. We pray that they will soon realize that God, you can neither leave them nor forsake them. We ask specifically that, Lord, under the light of your glory, they will begin to see the end of the wicked and thereby put their faith only in you. All these we ask in Jesus' name, Amen!

Prayer Power

Nothing shall separate us from the love of God…

11 LEAVING TO CLEAVE

Text: Mark 10: 1-12

" And he arose from thence, and cometh into the coasts of Judea by the farther side of Jordan: and the people resort unto him again; and, as he was wont, he taught them again. And the Pharisees came to him, and asked him, is it lawful for a man to put away his wife? tempting him. And he answered and said unto them, what did Moses command you? And they said, Moses suffered to write a bill of divorcement, and to put her away. And Jesus answered and said unto them, for the hardness of your heart he wrote you this precept. But from the beginning of the creation God made them male and female. For this cause shall a man leave his father and mother and cleave to his wife; and they twain shall be one flesh: so then they are no more twain, but one flesh. What therefore God hath joined together, let not man put asunder. And in the house his disciples asked him again of the same matter. And he saith unto them, whosoever shall put away his wife, and marry another, committeth adultery against her. And if a woman shall put away her husband, and be married to another, she committeth adultery."

Today's Confession

I am thankful for my marriage. Because I understand that law binds the woman who has a husband to him so long as the man lives. I thank the Lord, because he hates divorce; and a woman or man who marries another while the partner lives, sins. I ask for grace to love the things that God loves and to hate the things that God hates. In Jesus' name…

Intercession

Today, we remember all the people in legal marriages. We pray that they will soon realize that God, you hate divorce and that it shall not be part of their vocabulary. We ask specifically that, Lord, by the power of your holy counsel those whose marriages have suffered shipwreck will be delivered soon. All these we ask in Jesus' name, Amen!

Prayer Power

Breaking the spirit of infidelity by fire and sword…Greater protections for children against illicit trade and traffic, destitution and neglect…

12 HELP MY UNBELIEF, LORD

Text: Mark 9: 23 and 24

" Jesus said unto him, if thou canst believe, all things are possible to him that believeth. And straightway the father of the child cried out, and said with tears, Lord, I believe; help thou mine unbelief."

Today's Confession

I thank my God because he exists, and he rewards those who diligently seek him. I will not be a fool by saying in my heart; there is no God! Although I know that there is none who understands, none who always does good, yet, I still trust in God. I will not be like Thomas who doubted. I will not demand to see before I can trust the Lord. I will not be faithless but believing. The Lord is my God. And I am blessed because although I have not seen him, yet I believe. In Jesus' name…

Intercession

Today, we remember all those who doubt you simply because they don't have the physical or other forms of evidence. We pray that they will soon realize that God, you exist even if you cannot be seen with bare naked eyes. We ask specifically that, Lord, by the power of your living faith; that those who need to believe you for impossible situations, you will grant them the power to believe. All these we ask in Jesus' name, Amen!

Prayer Power

Salvation for the entire family; let our loved ones come to know Jesus…

Let all impossible situations become possible and bow before the power of your grace…

Let your power cancel debts, provide a cure for cancer and HIV/AIDS, bring Covid-19 under control, and end pillaging wars…

13 BE FILLED

Text: 1 Thess. 5: 18-20

" And be not drunk with wine, wherein is excess; but be filled with the Spirit; speaking to yourselves in psalms and hymns and spiritual songs, singing and making melody in your heart to the Lord; giving thanks always for all things unto God and the Father in the name of our Lord Jesus Christ."

Today's Confession

I have resolved that whether I eat or drink, or whatever I do; I will do all to the glory of God! I will not sleep as do others, but I will watch and be sober. For those who sleep, sleep in the night; and those who are drunk, get drunk in the night. Because I belong to the day, I will be sober, putting on the breastplate of faith and love; and a helmet of hope. I will not be drunk with wine in excesses but I will be filled with the Holy Spirit of promise. In Jesus' name…

Intercession

Today, we remember all those who are led astray by the effects of excessive alcohol and other intoxicating drinks or drugs. We pray that they will soon realize that God, you can set them free to come into the liberty of the Holy Church. We ask specifically that, Lord, by the power of your resurrection; all those who are addicted to intoxicating beverages or substance or psychotropic drugs abuse will be permanently set free. We pray that they will come to be filled with the Holy Spirit and with joy and thanksgiving. All these we ask in Jesus' name, Amen!

Prayer Power

Release for all those addicted to strong alcohol, narcotics, psychoactive drugs, and etc…

14 CHILDREN OF FREEDOM

Text: John 8: 34-36

" Jesus answered them, verily, verily, I say unto you, whosoever committeth sin is the servant of sin. And the servant abides not in the house forever: but the Son abides forever. If the Son therefore shall make you free, ye shall be free indeed."

Today's Confession

For me all things are lawful, but not all things are useful. Although all things are permissible to me, I will not be foolishly brought under the power of any. My body is the temple of the Holy Spirit, who is in me, and I am not my own. I was bought with a price; therefore, I will glorify God in my body and my spirit, which are God's. The Lord has searched me and known me. He knows my down sitting and my uprising and understands my thoughts from afar. The Lord safeguards my path and my lying down and is acquainted with all my ways. There is no word on my tongue which he does not know about. The Lord is on my side, whom shall I fear? I am God's child, free and not in bondage to anybody or anything. And that I will remain! In Jesus' name…

Intercession

Today, we remember all those who are bound by sin. We pray that they will soon realize that God, you have already translated them from the kingdom of darkness into the Kingdom of Light of your Son, our Lord Jesus Christ. We ask specifically that, Lord, by the power of your grace; all those who are blinded by the deceit of this life will be lifted from their blindness. We pray that they will come to the light of life and enjoy the freedom of the sons of light. All these we ask in Jesus' name, Amen!

Prayer Power

Binding the spirit of poverty and lack from among us in Jesus' name…

Opening up minds to realizing the blessedness of investments, entrepreneurship, economic enterprise, and etc…

15 DESIRE NO VAINGLORY

Text: Galatians 5:26

" Let us not be desirous of vainglory, provoking one another, envying one another."

Today's Confession

I will not be envious. I will not be bitter and I will not strive with any person in my heart. I will neither glorify myself nor speak against the truth. I understand that where envying and strife and confusion are, there evil abounds. I will sow seeds of righteousness in peace and rejoice with those who make peace. I will not desire any glory in vain but I will be contented. In Jesus' name…

Intercession

Today, we remember all those who are in the habit of praising themselves. We pray that they will soon realize that God, you are the one who lifts us from obscurity to glory. We ask specifically that, Lord, by the power of your grace, all those in need of the grace of humility will be granted. All these we ask in Jesus' name, Amen!

Prayer Power

Make my house visible in the land, O God…

16 PERISH NOT

Text: John 3:16

" For God so loved the world, that he gave his only begotten Son, that whosoever believeth in him should not perish, but have everlasting life."

Today's Confession

I believe in God and in Jesus Christ. I will not let my heart be troubled because I have a place in God's house. I am hopeful because I believe in God. That one-day God shall wipe away our tears from our eyes, and there shall be no more death, sorrow or crying. In life or in death, I will not be afraid, because though I walk through the valley of the shadow of death, God is with me. His rod and staff shall comfort me. And through the name of my God, I will not be lost. In Jesus' name…

Intercession

Today, we remember all those who are in danger of premature death. We pray that they will soon realize that God, those who place their hope in you, though they die, yet they shall live. We ask specifically that, Lord, by the abundance of your mercies, they will now acknowledge your great mercy and accept you in their hearts unto salvation. All these we ask in Jesus' name, Amen!

Prayer Power

Longevity is my portion; fruitfulness is my reward and favor is my experience in Jesus' name…

17 NEGLECT NOT YOUR PROFESSION

Text: Hebrews 4: 14-16

" Seeing then that we have a great high priest that is passed into the heavens, Jesus the Son of God, let us hold fast our profession. For we have not a high priest which cannot be touched with the feeling of our infirmities; but was in all points tempted like as we are yet, without sin. Let us therefore come boldly unto the throne of grace that we may obtain mercy and find grace to help in time of need."

Today's Confession

My heart and flesh will not faint because God is the strength of my heart and my portion forever. When I cry to God, he will hear my voice and get me out of trouble. In the night, I will not cease to seek after my God, and my soul will be comforted. I will remember my God and will not complain. O Lord, you see me rising up early in the morning and my plans are not far away from you. Sometimes I consider the old days and I am troubled. Sometimes I feel as if you have forsaken me. Other times I feel as though your promises towards me have failed. Lord, have you forgotten to be gracious to me? Have your anger shut up your tender mercies towards me? But as for me, I will not forget your works of love and your wonders of old. Because Lord you are a sun and shield to me, you have also become my grace and my glory. I am blessed in you and no good thing will you withhold from them who walk uprightly before you. I will not neglect my confession and profession, Lord. In Jesus' name…

Intercession

Today, we remember all those who are in danger of neglecting their faith. We pray that they will soon realize that God, you will not leave them nor sake them. We ask specifically that, Lord, you will comfort them in their hour of temptation and provide a way of escape. All these we ask in Jesus' name, Amen!

Prayer Power

Make us many, Sovereign God; from all directions let people come…

18 NO, NOT IN ISRAEL

Text: Matthew 8:5-11

"And when Jesus was entered into Capernaum, there came unto him a centurion, beseeching him, and saying, Lord, my servant lies at home sick of the palsy, grievously tormented. And Jesus saith unto him, I will come and heal him. The centurion answered and said, Lord, I am not worthy that thou should come under my roof: but speak the word only, and my servant shall be healed. For I am a man under authority, having soldiers under me: and I say to this man, go, and he goes; and to another, come, and he comes; and to my servant, do this, and he doeth it. When Jesus heard it, he marveled, and said to them that followed, verily I say unto you, I have not found so great faith, no, not in Israel."

Today's Confession

I will not worry about tomorrow. I will not worry

about my life: what I shall eat, drink or dress, because life is greater than food and the body more than clothes. The birds of the field don't sow or reap, yet, our heavenly Father feeds them. Rather, I will seek first God's kingdom and his righteousness, and all the things I want will be added unto me. In Jesus' name…

Intercession

Today, we remember all those who need lifesaving opportunities. We pray that they will soon realize that God, you will not cast out anyone that comes to you in simple faith. We ask specifically that, Lord, you will console all those who have lost their sources of livelihood due to downsizing, layoffs, retrenching or health reasons, that in the midst of all these your will shall prevail. All these we ask in Jesus' name, Amen!

Prayer Power

There will be plenty and to spare…may we overflow in all good things…

19 TO SEEK AND TO SAVE

Text: Luke 19:10

> "For the Son of man is come to seek and to save that which was lost."

Today's Confession

I will draw near to God with clean hands and a pure heart. I will not let my soul be cast down within me. I will hope in God because I will praise him for the help of his countenance. I will remember my God wherever I go. My soul is in deep turmoil like the deep of the mighty sea. I am like one who is drowning under many waters. Yet, the Lord will command his loving kindness in the daytime and in the night his song shall be with me. I will pray unto God, because he answers prayers, and will call upon him in truth! I will praise the LORD for his goodness and for his wonderful works to humanity. The Lord satisfies the longing of my soul and feeds my hungry soul with his goodness. O Lord, thank you because you came to seek and save the lost, and I was one of them! In Jesus' name…

Intercession

Today, we remember all those who are still under the lics of Satan, who are lost in sins and trespasses. We pray that they will soon realize that God, your arms are wide open and your eyes are open towards their coming back. We ask specifically that, Lord, you will send the gift of your servants who proclaim the good tidings of the Gospel of peace to them. As a result, they will hear the word of hope and repent of their wicked ways and be saved. All these we ask in Jesus' name, Amen!

Prayer Power

Release of souls for salvation; binding the spirit of apathy towards souls…
Freedom to live worthy lives before those who will see Christ in us…

20 I CAN DO ALL THINGS

Text: Phil. 4: 12 and 13

" I know both how to be abased, and I know how to abound: everywhere and in all things I am instructed both to be full and to be hungry, both to abound and to suffer need. I can do all things through Christ, which strengthens me."

Today's Confession

By the preaching of what seems to be the "foolishness" of the Gospel, many are saved. For people call for more, but God has chosen the foolishness of humanity to confound the wise. I will not need a sign except the cross of Jesus Christ. For to me, the preaching of the cross constitutes the power of God and the wisdom of God. I thank my Lord, because even his foolishness is wiser than the wisdom of the best of mankind, and his weakness, stronger than the mighty of military superiors! For me, the Lord Jesus is my wisdom, righteousness, sanctification and redemption. I glory in him because his grace to me is sufficient, and my strength is made perfect in weakness. Even more, I will rather glory in my infirmities that the power of Christ may rest upon me. Therefore, I take pleasure in infirmities, in reproaches, in necessities, in persecutions, in distress and in many trials. And I can do all things, great and small, complicated and simple, hard or difficult through Christ Jesus who gives me strength! In Jesus' name…

Intercession

Today, we remember all those who are weak due to disability, disaster, accident, calamity or catastrophe. We pray that they will soon realize that God, you are the help of the weak and the one who makes a way where there seems to be no way. We ask specifically that, Lord, you will provide a way out of their dilemma and sustain them in pain. May they come to know you as El-Shaddai, the Almighty God! All these we ask in Jesus' name, Amen!

Prayer Power

In the name of God, most gracious, most merciful: Thou shalt not touch my inheritance, Satan…there shall be no curse that shall land on my inheritance… no misfortune shall prevail over me…

21 SEVEN TIMES IN A DAY

Text: Luke 17: 3 and 4

"Take heed to yourselves: If thy brother trespasses against thee, rebuke him; and if he repents, forgive him. And if he trespasses against thee seven times in a day, and seven times in a day turns again to thee, saying, I repent; thou shalt forgive him."

Today's Confession

Even if at my first answer no man should stand with me, and even if all men should forsake me, yet I will pray to God, and I will not lay a charge against any person. This one thing I know, the Lord shall stand by me, and strengthen me. The lion will not devour me because the Lord shall deliver me from every evil work and will preserve me unto his heavenly kingdom. When my father and mother forsake me, then the Lord will take me up. The Lord shall teach me his ways and lead me in a plain path. The Lord shall not deliver me into the hands of my enemies nor will he allow the breath of the cruel near me. I would have fainted, but I believed I would see the goodness of the Lord in the land of the living. I will wait upon my God and be of good courage, and he shall strengthen my heart. I will also consider the poor, and so shall I be preserved and be kept alive. The Lord shall also bless me upon the earth and deliver me out of the languishing bed of sickness. The Lord shall heal my soul and preserve me from death. I will bless the Lord God of Israel from everlasting to everlasting. And I shall not hesitate to forgive seven times in a day. In Jesus' name…

Intercession

Today, we remember all those who have given up hope because of various challenges they are facing in life. We pray that they will soon realize that God, you can make their future better than their past. We ask specifically that, Lord, you will give them high self-esteem and heal them from all forms of depression. May they come to know you as Adonai, the LORD our Master! All these we ask in Jesus' name, Amen!

Prayer Power

My destiny is secure in Jesus' name…

22 THE PRAYER OF FAITH

Text: James 5: 14-16

"Is any sick among you? Let him call for the elders of the Church; and let them pray over him, anointing him with oil in the name of the Lord: And the prayer of faith shall save the sick, and the Lord shall raise him up; and if he has committed sins, they shall be forgiven him. Confess your faults one to another, and pray one for another, that ye may be healed. The effectual fervent prayer of a righteous man availeth much."

Today's Confession

I will not be angry lest my flesh be soundless. I will not sin and forfeit rest in my bones. As a heavy burden my iniquities went over my head. My wounds stunk because of my foolishness. I was troubled; I was bowed down greatly and I went mourning all day long. My loins were filled with a loathsome disease; I was feeble and roared and groaned on my bed. My heart panted and my strength fainted. As for the light of my eyes, it was gone from me. But I am poor and sorrowful; let your salvation, O God, set me up on high. I will praise the name of the Lord with a song; I will magnify him with thanksgiving. I will instruct my soul to glorify the Lord, and my heart to bless his holy name. My soul shall bless the Lord and will not forget all his benefits. The LORD forgives all my iniquities, heals all my diseases, redeems my life from destruction, crowns me with love and mercy, and delivers me from death. In Jesus' name…

Intercession

Today, we remember all those with incurable diseases. We pray that they will soon realize that God, with you, all things are possible. We ask specifically that, Lord, you will sustain them in their illness and provide them with supernatural and uncommon healing power. May they come to know you as Jehovah-Rapha, the LORD our Healer! All these we ask in Jesus' name, Amen!

Prayer Power

Miracles are in the air…we claim mighty miracles for …

23 WHAT MANNER OF A MAN IS THIS?

Text: Mark 4:37-41

"And there arose a great storm of wind, and the waves beat into the ship, so that it was now full. And he was in the hinder part of the ship, asleep on a pillow; and they awake him, and say unto him, master, carest thou not that we perish? And he arose, and rebuked the wind, and said unto the sea, peace, be still. And the wind ceased, and there was a great calm. And he said unto them, why are ye so fearful? How is it that ye have no faith? And they feared exceedingly, and said one to another, what manner of man is this, that even the wind and the sea obey him?"

Today's Confession

No man can harm me because I am a follower of good; and Christ is good! Even if I am meant to suffer for righteousness' sake, happy I am. I will not be afraid of my enemy's terror and will not be troubled by it. The Lord is my light and salvation; whom shall I fear? The Lord is the strength of my life; of whom shall I be afraid? When my enemies come upon me, they will stumble and fall. Though a troop should camp against me, in this will I be confident: The LORD is on my side; I will not fear. The Lord takes my part with those who help me. Therefore, I shall see my desire upon those who hate me. I would rather trust in the LORD than put my confidence in people. I would rather trust in the Lord than put my confidence in human beings. In Jesus' name…

Intercession

Today, we remember all those whose confidence is in other people. We pray that they will soon realize that God, you are the only hope they have. We ask specifically that, Lord, you will show them that people are of but a limited expanse: today they are and tomorrow are gone. May they come to know you as the everlasting God! All these we ask in Jesus' name, Amen!

Prayer Power

Enlarge my territory, dear Lord…and bless me indeed…
Open all good doors that must be opened; close all bad doors that should be closed …

24 AN EXAMPLE TO FOLLOW

Text: 1 Peter 2: 20-23

"For what glory is it, if, when ye be buffeted for your faults, ye shall take it patiently? But if, when ye do well, and suffer for it, ye take it patiently, this is acceptable with God. For even hereunto were ye called: because Christ also suffered for us, leaving us an example, that ye should follow his steps: Who did no sin, neither was guile found in his mouth: who, when he was reviled, reviled not again; when he suffered, he threatened not; but committed himself to him that judges righteously."

Today's Confession

I am aware that those who trouble me have increased. I am aware that they rise up against me. I am aware that many are there who say of my soul: there is no help for him or her in the LORD. But you LORD, you are my shield, my glory and the lifter up of my head. Each time I cry to you, you hear me out of your holy hill. This is the reason why I lay down and sleep and I wake up again, because the Lord sustains me.

Of a thousand of people that have set themselves against me around, I will not be afraid. My confidence is in this: my God will arise to save me! Salvation belongs to the Lord. Blessings are upon God's people. I love you Lord; your words also are smoother than butter and softer than oil. I will cast my burden upon you; you will sustain me. You shall not suffer me to be moved. You have set me as an example for others to follow! In Jesus' name…

Intercession

Today, we remember all those who have no direction in life and no good examples to follow. We pray that they will soon realize that God, you can lead and guide them to greener pastures. We ask specifically that, Lord, you will bring up good Christian models in our time that will lead by example and be imitators of Christ. All these we ask in Jesus' name, Amen!

Prayer Power

Good Christians in positions of influence…in government, decision-making, and etc…

25 SAVE US FROM LIES

Text: John 8:44

" Ye are of your father the devil, and the lusts of your father ye will do. He was a murderer from the beginning, and abode not in the truth, because there is no truth in him. When he speaks a lie, he speaks of his own: for he is a liar, and the father of lies."

Today's Confession

God our Father is true and his ways are truth. I am for the truth and I put away lying in order to speak the truth with all my neighbors. I know that the fearful, the unbelievers, the abominable, murderers, whole mongers, sorcerers, idolaters and all liars, shall have their part in the lake of fire which burns with fire and brimstone. I will not be among them because I have put on Christ and his will I do. In Jesus' name…

Intercession

Today, we remember all the victims of Satan's lies. We pray that they will soon realize that God, without you, they have no power to come into the knowledge of the truth. We ask specifically that, Lord, you will remove the cover of darkness off their eyes that they may see the light of your glorious Gospel. May they come to know you as the way, the truth and the life! All these we ask in Jesus' name, Amen!

Prayer Power

Financial breakthroughs, powerful financial opportunities, grace to prosper, financial independence…

26 SUP WITH ME

Text: Revelation 3: 20

"Behold, I stand at the door, and knock: if any man hears my voice, and opens the door, I will come in to him, and will sup with him, and he with me."

Today's Confession

The LORD is my shepherd; I shall not lack. He makes me to lie down in fresh, tender green pastures. He leads me besides the still and restful waters. He refreshes and restores my life. He leads me in the paths of uprightness for His names' sake. Even though I walk through the dark valley of the shadow of death, I will dread no evil, for he is with me. Besides, he protects me with his rod and comforts me with his staff. He also prepares food before me in the midst of famine and adversity; he anoints my head with oil, and my brimming cup runs over. Surely, only goodness, mercy and love shall follow me all the days of my life, and through the length of my days his house and presence shall be my dwelling place. In Jesus' name…

Intercession

Today, we remember all those who are jobless. We pray that they will soon realize that chances and opportunities belong to you. We ask specifically that, Lord, you will connect them to potential employers and favor them in their job searches and interviews. May they come to know you as Jehovah-Rohi, the LORD our Shepherd! All these we ask in Jesus' name, Amen!

Prayer Power

Angelic visitations…release of divine ideas…above all others and not below…heads and not tails…

27 AS UNTO THE LORD

Text: Colossians 3: 17, 23

" " And whatsoever you do in word or deed, do all in the name of the Lord Jesus, giving thanks to God and the Father by him. And whatsoever you do, do it heartily, as to the Lord, and not unto men."

Today's Confession

The Lord is my strong habitation to where I continually resort. He has given commandment to save me, for he is my rock and my fortress. Nothing I do pleases him unless I do it in his will. I thank the Lord, that in whatsoever I will do or say, I am determined to do and say in his name. In Jesus' name…

Intercession

Today, we remember the voiceless. We pray that they will soon realize that God, you are defender of the feeble. We ask specifically that, Lord; you will speak for them when they are falsely accused. May they come to know you as Jehovah-Nissi, the LORD our Banner! All these we ask in Jesus' name, Amen!

Prayer Power

Silencing the spell…attacking the spirit of witchcraft…conquering all wicked spirits released against us in Jesus' name…

28 CALMER OF HEARTS

Text: John 14: 27

"Peace I leave with you, my peace I give unto you: not as the world gives, give I unto you. Let not your heart be troubled, neither let it be afraid."

Today's Confession

I have been justified by faith; therefore, I have peace with God through my Lord Jesus Christ. Through Christ also I have access by faith into this grace wherein I stand and rejoice in the hope of the glory of God. I keep rejoicing in the Lord again and again. I try to let my moderation be made known to all people because the Lord is near. I am worried about nothing, but in everything, by prayer and petitions, with thanksgiving, I make my requests known to God. This results in the peace of God that passes all understanding which guards my heart and mind through Christ Jesus. In Jesus' name…

Intercession

Today, we remember all the broken-hearted due to various reasons. We pray that they will soon realize that God, you are the mender of broken hearts. We ask specifically that, Lord you will turn their disappointments into appointments. May they come to know you as their best friend! All these we ask in Jesus' name, Amen!

Prayer Power

Flow healing blood into my system…attack every foreign substance in my body…through the stripes of Jesus Christ I am healed…

29 WHEN I PRAY

Text: Luke 11:1

" And it came to pass, that, as he [Jesus] was praying in a certain place, when he ceased, one of his disciples said unto him, Lord, teach us to pray, as John also taught his disciples."

Today's Confession

My Father in heaven, I honor your holy name. I am keen to see your kingdom come and your will to be done both in my life and in this world, just as it is in heaven. Each day, give me the portion of food and provision that belongs to me. Lord, forgive all my sins because I also do forgive all those who sin against me. I ask you not to lead me into temptations, rather, to deliver me from all evil.

Lord, I thank you because you always hear me when I pray and you always answer my prayers. Like when a friend comes to me at midnight, and says that he is in need of three loaves of bread. Although my door will be shut and my children will be asleep, yet because he is persistent, despite being a friend, I will rise up and give him. Lord, I will always ask you because you will always give me; I will seek, because I will always find. I will knock, and you will always open. Lord, my confidence is in the fact that, if I ask you for bread, you will not give me a stone; and if I ask you for a fish, you will not give me a snake or a scorpion.

Lord, I know that if I who is human knows how to give good gifts to my natural and adopted children, what about you, the Father of creation? All that I need is to ask you. Lord Jesus, I believe in you, and due to this, I will do greater works than you did because you've gone to be with the Father. The comfort I have is that whatever I will ask the Father though the name of Jesus, I will be granted. This will glorify the Father.

The self-assurance I have in God is that if I ask him for anything according to his will, he will hear me. And since I know that he hears me, in whatever I ask, I also know that I have the petition that I desire of him.

I will cry unto God with my mouth and extol the Lord with my tongue. But if I regard iniquity in my heart, he will not hear me. For sure God has heard me and attended to the voice of my prayer. Blessed be God who has neither turned away my prayer nor his mercy from me. In Jesus' name …

Intercession

Today, we remember all those who depend on the arm of flesh for their sustenance. We pray that they will soon realize that God answers prayer and that all that they have to do is ask the Father for anything through the name of Jesus. We ask specifically that, Lord, you will grant them the desire and confidence to pray.

Father, we know that even though human agents may provide to us what we prayed for, it is God who both hears prayers and sends answers. It is God who parts the heavens and brings to us the benefits of our intercessions. It is God who hears when his children call unto him.

It is you, dear Father, who soothes your people and delivers them from all their enemies. It is you who is near to those who are afflicted. You are the Father of the fatherless and motherless. Hear us when we pray out of need, out of want, out of desperation, and out of joy. Be quick to send us help when we are beaten up, to defend us when we are wrongly accused, and to heal us when we are sick. Do, through us, miracles by stretching out your hand to cure, bless and make ways out of impossible situations. Work through time and come to our rescue within our time. May we come to know you as the God who answers prayer! All these we ask in Jesus' name, Amen!

Prayer Power

Power for supernatural ability to pray and see results…there will be no laziness as far as prayer is concerned…prayer a lifestyle and not a necessity…casting down the stronghold of prayerlessness in the Church…in Jesus' name…

30 AGAINST SUCH THERE IS NO LAW

Text: Galatians 5:19-23

" Now the works of the flesh are manifest, which are these; adultery, fornication…. But the fruit of the Spirit is love, joy, peace, longsuffering, gentleness, goodness, faith, meekness, temperance: against such there is no law."

Today's Confession

I know that the unrighteous shall not inherit the kingdom of God. I will not be deceived; fornicators, idolaters, adulterers, effeminates, abusers of themselves with mankind, thieves, covetous, drunkards, revellers, and extortionists shall not inherit the kingdom of God. I was once like them, but God washed me and sanctified me and justified me in the name of Jesus and by his Holy Spirit. Although I know that all things are lawful to me, I will not sin against God by disregarding the limits. Meats are for the belly, but if gluttony leads me to sin, God shall destroy them both in hell! My body is not for fornication, but for the Lord.

God's will for me is that I am sanctified and that I abstain from fornication. I am learning how to possess myself in sanctification and honor to the Lord. God has not called me to uncleanness, but to holiness. In Jesus' name…

Intercession

Today, we remember all those who are struggling with sin. We pray that they will soon realize that the grace of God that brings salvation has appeared to all men teaching them to say, "No!" to unrighteousness. We ask specifically that, Lord, you will deliver those who are addicted to sensual habits which fuel debauchery. All these we ask in Jesus' name, Amen!

Prayer Power

Praying against the spirit of immorality and pornography…uncleanness and filthy language from our lips…in Jesus' name…

Praying for a desire to live clean, free, right and loving…

31 I WILL INSTRUCT YOU

Text: Psalm 32:8

> "I will instruct thee and teach thee in the way which thou shalt go; I will guide thee with mine eye."

Today's Confession

By the mercies of the Lord, I present my body to God as a living sacrifice, holy and acceptable, which is my reasonable service. I will not be conformed to the pattern of this world but will be transformed by the renewing of my mind, that I may prove that which is God's good and acceptable and perfect will. O Lord, guide me to know in which way I should go so that my path may be straight! In Jesus' name…

Intercession

Today, we remember all those who are controlled by the dictates of this world system. We pray that they will soon realize that friendship with the evil is enmity with God. We ask specifically that, Lord, they will be in this world (supporting the good and defending God's creation) but not of this world (of the evil, debased and corrupt ways). All these we ask in Jesus' name, Amen!

Prayer Power

We shall believe the report of the Lord…thank God for medical doctors' reports, lawyers' representations, economists' indicators…and weather forecasts…but above all these…what the Lord says that shall prevail…

32 A LIGHT BURDEN

Text: Mathew 11:28

" "Come unto me, all you that labor and are heavy laden, and I will give you rest."

Today's Confession

I will run to God because there is safety with him. I will not burden myself with loads too heavy for me. The Lord will be my help and my deliverer. I will not labor in vain for what the Lord is not building. I will not keep in vain for which the Lord is not watching. I will not rise up early and sit up late, eat the bread of sorrows and lose sleep unless the Lord is with me. I am grateful to the Lord for all my children, biological, spiritual, adopted or otherwise. I am happy because God has blessed me with an inheritance. My enemies shall hear this and be ashamed. In Jesus' name…

Intercession

Today, we remember all the people who have been enslaved by others. We pray that they will soon realize that they are not slaves of anyone except slaves of righteousness. We ask specifically that, Lord, by the power of your Holy Ghost, they will be liberated to serve only you. All these we ask in Jesus' name, Amen!

Prayer Power

The spirit of righteousness and the fear of God…the spirit of holiness and purity…may our lives be a light and salt to the world…
Against the vagaries of historic slavery and colonialism…bigotry and racism…injustice and corruption…and against labor abuse and enslavement…

33 LOVE WORKS

Text: Romans 13:10

" Love works no ill to his neighbor: therefore love is the fulfilling of the law."

Today's Confession

I was once a violator of God's law but God changed me through grace by faith in Christ Jesus my Savior. Now I steal no more, but rather labor with my own hands that I may have enough to give to him that needs. My conversation is now without covetousness and I am content with such things as I have. Thank you, Lord, that you will never leave me nor forsake me. In Jesus' name…

Intercession

Today, we remember all the busybodies. We pray that they will soon realize that God, you bless hands that are busy doing something. We ask specifically that, Lord, you will move all of those who are idle so that they can contribute with their talents, abilities, and ideas. All these we ask in Jesus' name, Amen!

Prayer Power

A spirit of excellence…in everything…a spirit of diligent…exceptional ability to do and accomplish what we have begun…unconditional love for everyone, beginning with our families…

Grace to live according to grace and not according to Mosaic legalism…

34 KNOW YOU NOT

Text: 1 Corinthians 3: 16 and 17

"Know ye not that ye are the temple of God, and that the Spirit of God dwells in you? If any man defile the temple of God, him shall God destroy; for the temple of God is holy, which temple ye are."

Today's Confession

I will speak to my soul to be quiet when I am down cast. I will instruct my soul to hope in the Lord, for I shall yet praise him for the help of his countenance. I will remember the Lord from the land of adversity. I will seek the Lord early because he will save me from my powerful enemy. I will also praise the Lord because I am fearfully and wonderfully made; marvellous are his works! I will submit my body to God and give him thanks. I am the temple of God; he lives and makes his dwelling in my body. Therefore, I shall not give myself to abomination or pervasion, for in God I stand firm. In Jesus' name...

Intercession

Today, we remember all those who abuse their bodies in order to aggrandize their sensual lusts. We pray that they will soon realize that their bodies are not meant for sexual immorality but for the Lord. We ask specifically that all those involved in prostitution will receive God's grace to abstain and be saved. We pray that they will come to be filled with the Holy Spirit and give themselves to the service of God. All these we ask in Jesus' name, Amen!

Prayer Power

May we be filled with the Holy Spirit, …and power! May we beam in spiritual songs, new songs and melodies in our hearts to the Lord…

35 TRIUMPHANT IN CHRIST

Text: 2 Corinthians 2:14

"" Now thanks be unto God, which always causes us to triumph in Christ, and makes manifest the savor of his knowledge by us in every place."

Today's Confession

I will not be drunk with wine, wherein is excess; but I will be filled with the Spirit. I will speak to myself in psalms and hymns and spiritual songs, singing and making melody in my heart to the Lord. I will give thanks always for all things unto God and the Father in the name of our Lord Jesus Christ. I know that it is a good thing in my life to give thanks to God, and to sing praises unto his name. I will show forth the Lord's love in the mourning and his faithfulness in the night. With instruments also I will sing unto the Lord. I will magnify the Lord's name because he has made me glad through his works. I will triumph through the works of his hands. O Lord, how great are your works, and your thoughts are very deep towards me. I will make a joyful noise unto the Lord in this land, and I will serve my God with gladness. I will come before his presence with singing because I know that the Lord made me, and I am a lamb in his pasture. I will enter also into his gates with thanksgiving, and unto his courts with praise. I will be thankful unto him and I will bless his name. My God is good and his mercy is everlasting and his truth endures to all generations. In Jesus' name…

Intercession

Today, we remember all those who feel defeated by life's raging storms. We pray that they will soon realize that there is power in praise. We ask specifically that, Lord, by the power of thanksgiving; you will give them a spirit of joy, laughter and singing. We pray that they will come into the Holy Place with thanksgiving and into the Most Holy Place with praise. All these we ask in Jesus' name, Amen!

Prayer Point

Victory at all costs…no more falling…no more shipwreck…

36 I HAVE LEARNED CONTENTMENT

Text: Phil. 4:11

"Not that I speak in respect of want; for I have learned, in whatsoever state I am, therewith to be content. I know both how to be abased, and I know how to abound: everywhere and in all things I am instructed both to be full and to be hungry, both to abound and to suffer need. I can do all things through Christ who strengthens me."

Today's Confession

LORD, in you I will rest and wait patiently. I will not fret because of those who prosper dubiously. I will follow after King David who was young and then old but didn't see the righteous forsaken or their children begging for bread. I will be contented in whatever situation I am found. In Jesus' name...

Intercession

Today, we remember all those who fret by the success of others. We pray that they will soon realize that God, you are the owner of a cattle on a thousand hills, and all silver and gold belong to you. We ask specifically that, Lord, you will teach them to be contented and live within their means with joy. All these we ask in Jesus' name, Amen!

Prayer Power

Supernatural multiplication in numbers…may we continue to grow this year …

Joy to live within our means… patience to wait for our time to prosper…and grace to share with the poor and the needy…

37 BLESS THOSE WHO CURSE YOU

Text: Luke 6:27-28

" But I say unto you which hear, love your enemies, do good to them which hate you, bless them that curse you, and pray for them which despitefully use you."

Today's Confession

I have laid aside every weight and the sin that easily beset me, and I am running my spiritual race with patience. I always look to Jesus who is the originator and accomplisher of my belief system. I, like Jesus my Lord, despise the shame and race towards the cross for the upward calling of God in Christ Jesus. I consider my Lord who endured such contradiction of the sinful mob against him. I am ready even to suffer for my Lord's sake because Christ left me an example that I should follow. Jesus Christ did not sin, neither was guile found in his mouth. Who, even when he was reviled, never reviled back; when he suffered, he did not threaten, but committed himself unto God who judges righteously. Christ bore my sin in his body on the tree, that being dead to sins, I should live unto righteousness; and by whose stripes I am healed. For this reason, I bless and not curse, and may all the curses that are laid against me be turned into blessings. In Jesus' name…

Intercession

Today, we remember all those who are under the shadow of infertility. We pray that they will soon realize that God, you are the one who breaks curses and releases people from their miseries. We ask specifically that, Lord, by the power of heaven and of life, you will set them free to enjoy the beauty of parenting. All these we ask in Jesus' name, Amen!

Prayer Point

May our children see many good days and be wealthy in the land…we break the spirit of juvenile delinquency…we release the spirit of steadfastness…prosperity and fruitfulness…

May those who desire to conceive, conceive…those who desire to adopt, adopt… those who need a foster parent, find one…and all should find God as their loving Father…

38 BELIEVE...AND...RECEIVED

Text: John 1:12

> "But as many as *received* him, to them gave he power to become the sons of God, even to them that *believe* on his name." [Emphasis added]

Today's Confession

Dear Father,

The righteous and merciful God: As Moses lifted up the serpent in the wilderness, even so was Jesus lifted up on the cross, that whosoever believes in him should not perish but have eternal life. My God, you loved the world so much that you gave your only begotten Son that whosoever believes in him should not perish but have everlasting life. You did not send your Son into the world to condemn the world, but that the world through him might be saved. He who believes in him is not condemned: but he who does not believe is condemned already, because he has not believed in the only begotten Son of God. I believe on the Lord Jesus Christ, my family and I, and so we are saved. In Jesus' name…

Intercession

Today, we remember all the people in this world that are not yet saved by grace through faith in Christ Jesus. We pray that they will soon realize that God, you have already provided for their salvation through your dearest Son, our Lord Jesus Christ. We ask specifically that, Lord, you will cause them to come face to face with the truth of the Gospel of Christ, and to open their hearts to the Word of Life that is able to save their souls. We pray that they will believe in their hearts and confess what they believe with their mouth unto salvation. We, by the power of the Holy Ghost, lift the devil's blindness from their eyes and release them to believe and receive Jesus as their personal Lord and Savior. All these we ask in Jesus' name, Amen!

Prayer Power

Church, to love Jesus…and may God, Jesus Christ, fill every department with faithful workers…

39 WITNESSES TO PEOPLE

Text: Acts 1:8

" But ye shall receive power, after that the Holy Ghost is come upon you: and ye shall be witnesses unto me both in Jerusalem, and in all Judea, and in Samaria, and unto the uttermost parts of the earth."

Today's Confession

To the praise of God, the Father, who is the King eternal, immortal, invisible, the only wise God be the glory forever and ever. For him, and through him, and to him, are all things: to whom be glory forever. For who has the mind of the Lord, or who has been his counsellor? Or who has first given to him, and it shall be recompensed unto him again? For he has made us into witnesses unto all mankind of what we have heard and seen! The Lord be sanctified in our hearts, as we are ready always to answer to everyone who asks for a reason of our hope which is in our meekness and fear. Having a good conscience, that whereas people may speak evil of us, as evildoers, yet they may be ashamed to falsely accuse us because of our good conversation in Christ. O the depth of the riches both of the wisdom and knowledge of God! How unsearchable are his judgments, and his ways passed finding out! To him be power, glory, majesty and victory, forever and ever, Amen!

Intercession

Today, we pray that the whole world should come to acknowledge God's greatness, his invincibility and power. May the whole world bow and kneel before you, O Most High! That they may give you glory and honor, for you reign in power and light forever and ever, Amen!

Prayer Power

Count your blessings and name them one by one…thank God that you are alive and his light shines upon your life…

40 HE MUST INCREASE

Text: John 3:30-31

" He must increase, but I must decrease. He who cometh from above is above all: he who is of the earth is earthly, and speaketh of the earth: he who cometh from heaven is above all."

Today's Confession

Increase my faith, Lord Jesus! I am learning to have faith even as little as a mustard seed. I am confident in the Lord that I can say to a maple tree, "Be plucked by the root and get planted into the sea, and it shall obey me!" By my faith in the Lord, I can move mountains and cause impossible situations to succumb. In Jesus' name…

Intercession

    Today, we remember all the people who once shared our common faith in our Lord Jesus Christ, but who have now turned away to follow after vanity. We pray that they will soon realize that God, you stand from afar away waiting for their safe return to you. We ask specifically that, Lord, you will put the spirit of faith in them to know that however deep in sin they may have reached, your grace is sufficient to seek them out and reach them. All these we ask in Jesus' name, Amen!

Prayer Power

    Lord, decrease us as far as sin is concerned…but increase us abundantly in our numbers…and in righteousness…

41 GOD EXPANDS HIS PEOPLE

Text: 1 Corinthians 3: 6-7

" I have planted, Apollos watered; but God gave the increase. So then neither is he who planteth anything, neither he who watereth; but God who giveth the increase."

Today's Confession

Christ is my head; from him all the joints and bones of my life get their nourishment. God increases me. And the Lord will make me to increase and abound in love so that I can love other people more. Moreover, I will increase in my love for the Father who has loved me and given me consolation and good hope through grace. God will be merciful to me and will bless me. He will cause his face to shine upon me. Then I shall know him and his saving health among all nations. Through my life and actions, I will let people praise God and I shall cause the nations to be glad and sing with joy for him. The Lord is judge and governor of the nations. The Lord shall bless me and cause the earth to yield its increase, from this day forward. In Jesus' name…

Intercession

Today, we pray for the blessing of the nations. We pray that there will be peace and prosperity in those nations that have been torn apart by war. We ask specifically for the Middle East and Afghanistan to finally find peaceful resolution to the on-going conflicts between Israel and Palestine, and between the Talibans and the government, respectively. We intercede for the safety of Israel and the Jewish people so that our God can surround them as mountains surround Jerusalem. We intercede for Palestine so that God's favor can continue to shelter them. We pray for Zambia and Canada to continue to put God first. All these we pray in Jesus' name, our Savior, Amen!

Prayer Power

Release the people who are supposed to attend Church…in the mighty name of God, in Jesus' name…
Persuade governments and the international organizations to resolutely solicit and manage world peace, courageously and judiciously…

42 IN MY FATHER'S BUSINESS

Text: Luke 2:49-52

"And he said unto them, how is it that ye sought me? Wist ye not that I must be about my Father's business? And they understood not the saying that he spoke unto them. And he went down with them, and came to Nazareth, and was subject unto them: but his mother kept all these sayings in her heart. And Jesus increased in wisdom and stature, and in favor with God and man."

Today's Confession

The wise in heart shall be called prudent and the sweetness of their lips shall increase learning. A wise man is strong and a man of knowledge increases strength. I am rich and I increase in goods, and in Christ I have no need of anything. In Christ I am not wretched and I am not miserable. I am not poor, blind or naked. I take pleasure in doing my heavenly Father's business. I am fulfilled and glad. I walk worthy of the Lord unto all pleasing, being fruitful in every good work, and increasing in the knowledge of God and in grace. In Jesus' name…

Intercession

Today, we remember all those who are outside of the will of God. We pray that they will soon realize that the grace and presence of God bring tremendous contentment. We ask specifically that, Lord, you will help those you have called to the Gospel business to soon come to accept the call and function therein. All these we ask in Jesus' name, Amen!

Prayer Power

Give us wisdom so that we can distinguish right from wrong and make informed decisions in life…

43 THE WORD OF GOD GREW

Text: Acts 6:7

"And the word of God increased; and the number of the disciples multiplied in Jerusalem greatly; and a great company of the priests were obedient to the faith."

Today's Confession

May the Churches be established in faith and increase in numbers daily! May we not boast of things with our measure of other men's labors, but having hope when our faith increases, that the Lord shall enlarge us. May we preach the Gospel in the regions beyond us and not merely boast in other people's work made ready to us. We will glory only in the Lord. We will not commend ourselves according to the commendation of other people. We will not boast because of an increase in material possessions, but with every spiritual richness you freely grant us, we shall boast in the grace of God. The Lord shall increase us greatly and make us stronger than our enemies. In Jesus' name…

Intercession

Today, we remember all those who are unstable in their Church membership and attendances. We pray that they will soon realize that they need a home Church that can nurture and groom them in the ways of the Lord. We ask specifically that, Lord, they will find a faithful pastor to whom they will submit and who will give an eternal account of their deeds before the Father. All these we ask in Jesus' name, Amen!

Prayer Power

Give us the spirit of evangelism…so that we may spread the Word of God like wildfire…

44 JESUS IS PRECIOUS

Text: 1 Peter 2:1-7

"Wherefore laying aside all malice, and all guile, and hypocrisies, and envies, and all evil speaking, as newborn babes, desire the sincere milk of the word, that ye may grow thereby: If so ye have tasted that the Lord is gracious. To whom coming, as unto a living stone, disallowed indeed of men, but chosen of God, and precious, you also, as lively stones, are built up a spiritual house, a holy priesthood, to offer up spiritual sacrifices, acceptable to God by Jesus Christ. Wherefore also it is contained in the scripture, behold, I lay in Zion a chief corner stone, elect, precious: and he that believeth on him shall not be confounded. Unto you therefore who believe he is precious."

Today's Confession

I will grow in grace and in the knowledge of my Lord and Savior Jesus Christ. I will grow up unto him, to whom be glory both now and forever, by speaking the truth in love.

I will always thank my God for all my brethren, especially when I hear that their faith is growing exceedingly, and when their love towards each other is abounding much. The Lord is indeed precious to us who believe. In Jesus' name…

Intercession

Today, we remember all the men and women of God who are laboring hard to lead the flock of the Lord. We pray that they will execute their discharges with happiness and courage. We ask specifically that, Lord, by the power of your Holy Ghost, they will neither be discouraged nor abandon their flocks due to pressure or spiritual warfare. All these we ask in Jesus' name, Amen!

Prayer Power

Praise God for his greatness…worship him for his surpassing greatness…

Pray for faithful men and women to seek to lead God's flock without greed or corruption…

45 I WILL MULTIPLY YOU

Text: Hebrews 6: 13-15

"For when God made a promise to Abraham because he could swear by no greater, he swore by himself, saying, surely blessing I will bless thee, and multiplying I will multiply thee. And so, after he had patiently endured, he obtained the promise."

Today's Confession

I am blessed and fruitful. My seed is blessed and will multiply in the land so that we shall be many. My Church is blessed and shall multiply in this land and beyond. My possession will increase in the land and there will be no room for it. I will prosper beyond measure and be a good giver to godly causes. I will not decrease but only increase in every good thing as the Lord grants me favor each and every day. In Jesus' name…

Intercession

Today, we remember all the newly formed Churches in Canada, Zambia and beyond. We pray that they will rise up with the divine anointing of multiplication in numbers and in grace. We ask specifically that, Lord, you will abundantly multiply the number of all who are spreading the Good News to all nations, races, tribes and diversities. All these we ask in Jesus' name, Amen!

Prayer Power

Bind the spirit of the near-success syndrome…in your life and in the Church…release the spirit of completion of everything begun…

46 AT YOUR WORD

Text: Luke 5:4-5

"Now when he had left speaking, he said unto Simon, launch out into the deep, and let down your nets for a draught. And Simon answering said unto him, Master, we have toiled all the night, and have taken nothing: nevertheless at thy word I will let down the net."

Today's Confession

And the multitude of them that believed were of one heart and one soul. No one said of his or her things that they were his or hers only. But they had all things in common. By the grace of our God, we shall be gathered together a mighty multitude. We shall stand together of all nations, kindreds, peoples and tongues to glorify our God who reigns forever. We shall be a voice of a great multitude like the voice of a mighty thundering, saying, "Alleluia, for the Lord God Omnipotent reigns!" In Jesus' name…

Intercession

Today, we remember all those who are fruitless in their labors. We pray that they will soon realize that it is God who blesses the work of their hands. We ask specifically that they will be rewarded in their labors, which they labor day and night. All these we ask in Jesus' name, Amen!

Prayer Power

Reclaiming all that has been lost…whatever could not work yesterday or last year must work now…in Jesus' name…

47 ADD TO FAITH...

Text: 2 Peter 1:5-7

" And beside this, giving all diligence, add to your faith virtue; and to virtue knowledge; and to knowledge temperance; and to temperance patience; and to patience godliness; and to godliness brotherly kindness; and to brotherly kindness charity."

Today's Confession

And she called his name Joseph, and said, the Lord shall *add* to me another son. May the Lord our God add to us a hundredfold even as his grace as already given us all things. May we see many additions in our lifetime and give glory to God. The Lord shall also hear my prayers and add many years to my life. I will not die prematurely; rather, I shall live to see the fullness of my days. My health shall continue to perform, my strength will not reduce by the growing years and my faculties will remain sound even at an old age. The Lord will not forsake me even when I am old. Fruitfulness, power, and favor will characterize my life, and his goodness I shall live to see in the land of the living, all the days of my life. In Jesus' name…

Intercession

Today, we remember all those who are bereaved. We pray that they will soon realize that Jesus is the resurrection and the life. We ask specifically that, Lord, by the power of life; you will give them the spirit of endurance and courage to know that all will be fine again. All these we ask in Jesus' name, Amen!

Prayer Point

Our year of divine growth…excellence is our portion…may we be better than our competitors…

48 SINGLENESS OF HEART

Text: Acts 2:46-47

"And they continuing daily with one accord in the temple, and breaking bread from house to house, did eat their meat with gladness and singleness of heart, praising God, and having favor with all the people. And the Lord added to the Church daily such as should be saved."

Today's Confession

The Lord shall add to us multitudes both of men and women. The Lord has made us good men and women and filled us with the Holy Spirit and faith. We have received his Word freely and we have undergone his baptism with joy. Thousands of souls will be added to us because the Lord has meant good for us. We are of those who continue in the house of our God, seeking after him and beholding his beauty day in and day out. Souls who will later be saved shall also be added unto our congregation. Although our beginning was small, yet, our later end shall greatly increase.

We shall not despise small beginnings but we will rejoice with what the Lord is doing in our midst. In Jesus' name…

Intercession

Today, we remember the double-minded people all over the world. We pray that they will soon realize that God, you are the one who removes hearts of stone and gives hearts of flesh. We ask specifically that, Lord you will teach them to be men and women of integrity. All these we ask in Jesus' name, Amen!

Prayer Power

Breaking generation curses…the sins and mistakes of our forefathers will not haunt us…we disassociate ourselves from their evil legacy and claim the precious victory brought to us through the blood of our Lord Jesus Christ…

49 AN EXCELLENT SPIRIT

Text: Daniel 6:3

"Then this Daniel was preferred above the presidents and princes, because an excellent spirit was in him; and the king thought to set him over the whole realm."

Today's Confession

I have sound reasoning, sanity and dignity. I am well established in the kingdom of my God and the majesty of the kingdom is mine in Christ. The excellence of power and the excellence of distinction are of the children of God. God's excellence makes me bored. Through his excellence I mount up to the heavens and claim my place in Christ. My God decks himself with majesty and excellence and arrays himself with glory and beauty! His voice reverberates in the universe and awakes all humanity from its dubious ways. He rides on the wings of the wind and seats suspended on a crystal sea. His beauty is indescribable; his power, unfathomable; and his glory, unapproachable. Surely God is great, and most worthy of worship! In Jesus' name…

Intercession

Today, we remember all those who are self-proclaimed atheists and heretics. We pray that they will soon realize that there is only one true God, revealed in God the Father, the Son, and the Holy Ghost. We ask specifically that, Lord, by your eternal mercies and grace, you will command your steadfast love to such people in showing them that all other grounds they stand on are but sinking sand. All these we ask in Jesus' name, Amen!

Prayer Point

When the righteous are in power, the city rejoices; but when the wicked reigns there is no shout of joy…make us rulers and leaders in legislatures and executive branches…cause us to rise as great managers of human affairs…to be formidable magistrates and decision-makers…

50 THE SUPERIORITY OF WISDOM

Text: 1 Kings 4:30-34

"And Solomon's wisdom excelled the wisdom of all the children of the east country, and all the wisdom of Egypt. For he was wiser than all men; than Ethan the Ezrahite, and Heman, and Chalcol, and Darda, the sons of Mahol: and his fame was in all nations round about. And he spoke three thousand proverbs: and his songs were a thousand and five. And he spoke of trees, from the cedar tree that is in Lebanon even unto the hyssop that springeth out of the wall: he spoke also of beasts, and of fowl, and of creeping things, and of fishes. And there came of all people to hear the Wisdom of Solomon, from all kings of the earth, which had heard of his wisdom."

Today's Confession

I will bless the Lord who excels in strength. I will zealously seek the Lord my God for his excellence is over his people, and his strength is in the heavens. I shall blossom and rejoice with joy and singing. The glory of mighty nations shall be given unto the meek, and men will be forced to seek the glory of the Lord. O Lord our God, you have increased us in wisdom and prudence far above our adversary. You have made us more favorable than those who hold posts. We need not be afraid of who we don't know, because we know you, O God, Most High. In Jesus' name…

Intercession

Today, we remember all the people in this world who are oppressed by dictatorial regimes. We pray that they will soon realize that God, you love them and you are planning for their release from bondage. We ask specifically that, Lord you will raise men and women in such nations that know and fear you to take over leadership and provide a free atmosphere of peace, the rule of law and equity. All these we ask in Jesus' name, Amen!

Prayer Power

Declare favor…there shall be no bad luck among God's people…

51 SWEET INFLUENCES

Text: Job 38:31

"Canst thou bind the sweet influences of Pleiades, or loose the bands of Orion?"

Today's Confession

I am an influencer; a persuader of men and women to seek, love and serve Jehovah God. I will persuade all men to become good and to embrace the things that concern God. I will boldly declare the requirements of God and spread the sweet aroma of his goodness. I will rejoice with those who do righteousness and expose all the works of darkness. I will defend the faith and promote the good news of the Gospel of peace. I am not ashamed of the Gospel because it is the power of God to all who believe. I will endure afflictions as a good soldier of the cross and thereby exhort the sweet influences of my God. In Jesus' name…

Intercession

Today, we pray against the spread of false religions! We intercede that they will be unveiled and be revealed for what they are. We ask specifically, that Lord you will rise as a Man of war and put evil to shame. All these we ask in Jesus' name, our Savior, Amen!

Prayer Power

Give us people…give us souls…for influence…in Jesus' name…
Give us resources…give us finances so that we can build your kingdom…Amen!

52 ALL OF GRACE

Text: John 1:14

"And the Word was made flesh, and dwelt among us, (and we beheld his glory, the glory as of the only begotten of the Father,) full of grace and truth."

Today's Confession

God's Word, from cover to cover, is a message of your grace. In times past, O God, you treated us according to the law. Now, you have dealt with us according to your grace. We did not deserve anything from you. All we deserved was punishment and death. But in your righteous grace, you provided a perfect sacrifice through your holy Son, our Lord, Jesus Christ. He had not wronged you and let alone offending you. He had no fault, no sin in him. He treated everyone lovingly. He was grace incarnate. Yet, him we punished, disgraced, degraded, crucified and killed. O LORD, it was for our sake that our Lord died. It was for our sake that he rose again from the dead on the third day. Through him, we have received grace, first, to save us from hell and death, and second, to give us free access to the Father, and last, to help us in all of our life endeavours. It is all of grace, not of our initiative, intelligence, wisdom, wit or sophistication; it is all of his grace that we are saved and have inherited all good things, in heaven and on earth. In Jesus' name...

Intercession

Today, we pray against intolerance in the Body of Christ. Yes, we are not to tolerate evil and sin. Yes, we are not to tolerate anything that denies that Jesus Christ is the Son of God, and that he lived and died, and that on the third day, he rose again from the dead. But we must tolerate those who do not believe or are blinded by the evil arm of the devil. We intercede that we, the Body of Christ, will love all people irrespective of their religious affiliation or sin. We shall not fear to associate with them for Jesus' sake. For we, ourselves, are but sinners only forgiven. We ask specifically, that Lord you will raise in the Church men and women and the youth who will not be ashamed of the Gospel, who will not shy away from associating with sinners, tax collectors and the diseased. That they will eat and dine with all manner of people and they shall be used of God to save some. All these we ask in Jesus, our Savior's name, Amen!

Prayer Power

Give us love...give us courage...to meet people where they are comfortable...in Jesus' name...
Give us the spirit of tolerance...give us wisdom to see the truth and to have the right judgment...Amen!

ABOUT THE AUTHOR

CHARLES MWEWA

Charles Mwewa (LLM – cand.) is a Dad, a husband, a prolific author and researcher, poet, novelist, political thinker, a law professor, and Christian and community leader. Mwewa has written no less than 30 books and counting. Mwewa, his wife and their three daughters, reside in the Canadian Capital City of Ottawa.

AUTHOR'S CONTACT

Email address:

spynovel2016@gmail.com

Facebook:

www.facebook.com/charlesmwewa

Twitter:

https://twitter.com/BooksMwewa

Instagram:

instagram.com/mwewabooks/?hl=en

Author's website:

https://www.charlesmwewa.com

To order this book online:

www.amazon.com

INDEX

A

abilities, 70
abominable, 51
Abraham, 93
access, 57, 107
accident, 42
acknowledge, 8, 10, 34, 82
Adonai, 44
adopt, 78
adulterers, 16, 63
adultery, 23, 63
adversary, 104
Afghanistan, 86
agents, 61
agreement, iv
alcohol, 28
Almighty God, 42
Amen, 2, 4, 6, 8, 11, 14, 16, 18, 20, 22, 24, 26, 28, 30, 32, 34, 36, 38, 40, 42, 44, 46, 48, 50, 52, 54, 56, 58, 61, 64, 66, 68, 70, 72, 74, 76, 78, 80, 84, 86, 88, 90, 92, 94, 96, 98, 100, 102, 104, 106, 108
anointing, 45, 94
answers, 39, 61
Apollos, 85
Apostle Paul, iv
archangel, 6
arrogance, 20
associating, 108
asunder, 15, 23
atheists, 102
authority, 37

B

baptism, 99
beauty, 78, 99, 101
believers, v, 10
belly, 9, 63
benefits, 46, 61
best friend, 58
Bible, ii, iii, iv
bigotry, 68
blessings, 2, 78, 82
blood, 2, 4, 10, 11, 58, 100
boast, 89
body, 15, 29, 38, 58, 63, 65, 71, 78
Body of Christ, 108
bondage, 14, 30, 104
bones, 11, 45, 85
bread, 9, 59, 67, 75, 99
breastplate, 27
brethren, 13, 21, 92
broken-hearted, 6, 58
burden, 11, 20, 45, 50, 67
business, 87, 88
butter, 50

C

calamity, 3, 42
calm, 1, 47
Canada, ii, 86, 94
catastrophe, 42
cattle, 76
centurion, 37
Chalcol, 103
chances and opportunities, 54

charity, 97
children, 24, 59, 60, 61, 67, 75, 78, 101, 103
Christ, i, 6, 7, 10, 14, 15, 17, 20, 27, 30, 33, 40, 41, 47, 49, 50, 51, 57, 58, 69, 73, 75, 77, 80, 82, 84, 85, 87, 91, 100, 101, 107, 108
Christian, 50, 109
Christians, 22, 50
Church, 15, 28, 45, 62, 80, 86, 90, 93, 94, 99, 108
clean, 10, 11, 39, 64
cleave, 15, 23
colonialism, 68
comfort, 6, 19, 33, 36, 60
commandment, 55
compassion, 9
competitors, 98
conceive, 10, 78
confessions, ii
confidence, 48, 50, 60, 61
confusion, 31
congregation, iii, iv, v, 99
conscience, 82
consolation, 85
contempt, 11
contented, 31, 75, 76
contentment, 88
conversation, 69, 82
convict, 11
corruption, 68, 92
counsellor, 81
country, 9, 103
courage, 44, 92, 98, 108
covetous, 63
covetousness, 69
Covid, 6, 26
criticism, 8
cross, 41, 77, 79, 105
curse, 42, 77, 78

D

Daniel, 101
Darda, 103
darkness, 8, 10, 30, 52, 105
death, 5, 12, 14, 33, 34, 44, 46, 53, 107
debauchery, 64
decision, 50, 102
defender, 56
deliverer, 67
department, 80
depression, 44
desperation, 61
destiny, 44
devotion, v
dictatorial regimes, 104
disability, 42
disappointments, 58
disciples, 23, 59, 89
distinction, 101
diversities, 94
divorce, 24
doctors, 66
doors, 48
double-minded people, 100
downsizing, 38
drugs, 28
drunkards, 63

E

economic enterprise, 30
economists, 66
El-Shaddai, 42
employers, 54
enemies, 3, 19, 43, 48, 61, 67, 77, 89
enslavement, 68
entrepreneurship, 30
envying, 31
escape, 36

Ethan, 103
evangelism, 90
evidence, 26
evil, 3, 10, 17, 19, 31, 43, 53, 59, 66, 82, 91, 100, 106, 108
evildoers, 82
example, 17, 49, 50, 77
excellence, 70, 98, 101, 103
excellent spirit, 101
executive, 102
extortionists, 63
eye, 7, 65
Ezra, iii

F

faith, 1, 2, 4, 21, 22, 26, 27, 36, 37, 38, 45, 47, 57, 63, 69, 80, 83, 84, 89, 92, 97, 99, 105
faithful, 5, 10, 80, 90, 92
faithfulness, 73
faithless, 25
false religions, 106
family, 16, 26, 80
famine, 9, 53
Father, 3, 10, 11, 27, 38, 51, 55, 59, 60, 61, 73, 78, 79, 81, 85, 87, 90, 102, 107
fatted calf, 10
faults, 10, 11, 45, 49
favor, 34, 54, 86, 87, 93, 98, 99, 104
fear, 2, 15, 30, 47, 68, 82, 104, 108
fellowship, 10
finances, 106
financial independence, 52
financial opportunities, 52
fire, 24, 51
flesh, 2, 15, 23, 35, 45, 61, 63, 100, 107
flocks, 92
food, 38, 53, 59
fool, 25

foolishness, 41, 45
foreign, 58
forgive, 3, 10, 11, 18, 43, 44, 59
fornication, 63
forsaken, 21, 36, 75
fortress, 2, 55
foster parent, 78
free, 8, 11, 28, 29, 30, 64, 78, 104, 107
freedom, 14, 30
friendship, 66

G

generations, 74
gladness, 11, 74, 99
glory, 6, 8, 22, 27, 31, 32, 36, 41, 49, 57, 81, 82, 89, 91, 97, 101, 103, 107
gluttony, 63
godliness, 97
gold, 76
Good News, 94
good things, 38, 108
goodness, 11, 16, 39, 44, 53, 63, 98, 105
Gospel, 40, 41, 52, 80, 88, 89, 105, 108
government, 50, 86
governor, 85
grace, 24, 26, 30, 32, 35, 36, 41, 52, 57, 64, 69, 70, 72, 76, 80, 84, 85, 88, 89, 91, 94, 95, 97, 102, 107
greed, 92

H

habitation, 3, 55
habits, 64
happiness, 92
heads and not tails, 54
Healer, 46

health, 38, 85, 97
heart, 6, 8, 11, 19, 23, 25, 27, 31, 33, 35, 39, 44, 45, 57, 60, 73, 87, 95, 99
heaven, 5, 6, 8, 9, 19, 59, 78, 83, 108
hell, 63, 107
Heman, 103
heretics, 102
hill, 49
HIV/AIDS, 26
holiness, 64, 68
holy, 5, 10, 13, 16, 24, 46, 49, 59, 65, 71, 91, 107
Holy Ghost, 68, 80, 81, 92, 102
Holy God, 11
Holy Place, 74
Holy Spirit, 6, 11, 18, 27, 28, 29, 63, 72, 99
honor, 15, 59, 64, 82
hope, 6, 27, 34, 39, 40, 44, 48, 57, 71, 82, 85, 89
house, 23, 29, 32, 33, 54, 91, 99
humanity, 39, 41, 101
humiliation, 15
humility, 20, 32
hunger, 9
husband, 5, 15, 24, 109
hymns, 27, 73
hypocrisy, 13
hypocrite, 7

I

ideas, 54, 70
idolaters, 51, 63
imitators, 50
immorality, 64, 72
impossible situations, 4, 26, 61, 83
imprisonment, 8
infertility, 78
infidelity, 24
influence, 50, 106

inheritance, 42, 67
iniquity, 10, 60
initiative, 107
injustice, 8, 68
insecurities, 20
instruments, 73
integrity, 100
intelligence, 107
intercessions, ii, 61
international organizations, 86
interviews, 54
intoxicating drinks, 28
investments, 30
invocations, ii, iii
Israel, iii, 37, 44, 86

J

Jehovah-Nissi, 56
Jehovah-Rapha, 46
Jehovah-Rohi, 54
Jerusalem, 81, 86, 89
Jesus, 2, 3, 4, 6, 7, 8, 10, 11, 13, 14, 16, 17, 18, 19, 20, 22, 23, 24, 25, 26, 27, 28, 29, 30, 31, 32, 33, 34, 35, 36, 37, 38, 40, 41, 42, 44, 46, 48, 50, 51, 52, 54, 55, 56, 57, 58, 59, 60, 61, 62, 63, 64, 65, 66, 67, 68, 69, 70, 71, 72, 73, 74, 75, 76, 77, 78, 79, 80, 83, 84, 86, 87, 88, 89, 90, 91, 92, 93, 94, 96, 98, 100, 102, 104, 105, 106, 107, 108
Jewish people, 86
job, 54
jobless, 54
John, 5, 29, 33, 51, 57, 59, 79, 83, 107
Jordan, 23
Joseph, 97
joy, 8, 10, 28, 61, 63, 74, 76, 85, 99, 102, 103
Judea, 23, 81
judge, 7, 10, 85

judgment, 7, 8, 108
juvenile delinquency, 78

K

kindness, 10, 11, 39, 97
King David, 75
knowledge, 52, 73, 82, 87, 91, 97

L

labor, 67, 68, 69, 96
lamb, 74
land, 9, 32, 42, 44, 71, 74, 78, 93, 98
language, 64
laughter, 74
law, 8, 24, 63, 69, 104, 107, 109
lawyers, 66
layoffs, 38
laziness, 62
lead, 19, 43, 50, 59, 92
leaders, 102
leadership, 104
Lebanon, 103
legacy, 100
legislatures, 102
liar, 51
liberty, 14, 28
lie, 10, 51, 53
lies, 37, 40, 51, 52
life, 16, 30, 33, 38, 44, 46, 48, 50, 52, 53, 59, 73, 74, 78, 79, 82, 85, 88, 94, 97, 98, 107
lifestyle, 62
lion, 43
lips, 64, 87
litany, ii
lost, 10, 16, 33, 38, 39, 40, 96
lots, 3
love, 11, 16, 21, 22, 24, 27, 36, 46, 50, 54, 63, 69, 70, 73, 77, 80, 85, 91, 102, 104, 105, 108

lusts, 16, 51, 72

M

magistrates, 102
malice, 91
managers, 102
marriage, 15, 16, 24
Master, 1, 44, 95
material possessions, 89
matrimony, 16
meekness, 63, 82
mercy, 10, 13, 34, 35, 46, 53, 60, 74
merry, 10
Middle East, 86
midnight, 59
military, 41
milk, 91
mind, 6, 13, 57, 65, 81
misfortune, 6, 42
mistakes, 100
moderation, 57
morning, 19, 35
Mosaic legalism, 70
Moses, 23, 79
most gracious, 42
Most Holy Place, 74
most merciful, 42
mountains, 83, 86
mourning, 45, 73
mouth, 17, 49, 60, 77, 80
murderer, 51

N

narcotics, 28
nations, 85, 86, 94, 95, 103, 104
Nazareth, 87
necessities, 42
neighbors, 51
new earth, 5
New Jerusalem, 5

nourishment, 85
numbers, 76, 84, 89, 94

O

offences, 11
oil, 45, 50, 53
Omnipotent, 96
Orion, 105

P

pain, 5, 42
Palestine, 86
pandemics, 6
partner, 15, 24
pastures, 50, 53
path, 29, 43, 65
patience, 76, 77, 97
peace, 1, 14, 31, 40, 47, 57, 63, 86, 104, 105
perfect will, 13, 65
perish, 1, 9, 33, 47, 79
persecutions, 42
persistent, 59
pervasion, 71
petitions, 57
Pharisees, 23
pigs, 9
pillow, 1, 47
pleasing, 87
Pleiades, 105
poor, 44, 45, 76, 87
pornography, 64
portion, 9, 34, 35, 59, 98
power, 2, 18, 24, 26, 28, 29, 30, 32, 41, 46, 52, 68, 72, 74, 78, 79, 80, 81, 82, 92, 98, 101, 102, 105
praise, 8, 39, 46, 71, 74, 81, 85
prayer, 45, 57, 60, 61, 62
prayerlessness, 62
prayers, 16, 18, 39, 59, 61, 97
presence, 11, 54, 74, 88
presidents, 101
pride, 20
priest, 35
profession, 35, 36
promise, 27, 93
prosperity, 78, 86
prostitution, 72
proverbs, 103
prudence, 104
psychoactive, 28
psychotropic, 28
public, iv
purpose, 21

R

races, 94
racism, 68
relationships, 15
repent, 40, 43
resolution, 86
resources, 106
rest, 42, 45, 67, 75
resurrection, 28, 98
revellers, 63
revival, 6
riches, 82
righteousness, 31, 38, 41, 47, 68, 78, 84, 105
ring, 10
robe, 10
rock, 19, 55
rod and staff, 33

S

sacrifice, 13, 65, 107
safety, 67, 86
salvation, 11, 19, 34, 40, 46, 47, 64, 80
Samaria, 81

sanctification, 16, 41, 64
Satan, 2, 4, 40, 42, 52
Savior, 15, 69, 80, 86, 91, 106, 108
scorpion, 60
sea, 1, 5, 39, 47, 83, 101
seed, 83, 93
self-assurance, 60
self-esteem, 44
servants, 9, 40
service, 13, 65, 72
shepherd, 53
ship, 1, 47
shipwreck, 24, 74
shoes, 10
sickness, 44
silver, 76
Simon, 95
sin, 10, 11, 17, 29, 30, 35, 45, 49, 59, 63, 64, 77, 84, 107, 108
slavery, 68
slaves, 8, 68
sleep, 27, 49, 67
snake, 60
sober, 27
soldiers, 37
Solomon, 103
Son of God, 35, 80, 108
sorcerers, 51
sorrow, 5, 6, 33
soul, 3, 13, 18, 19, 35, 39, 44, 46, 49, 71, 95
spell, 56
spirit of completion, 94
spiritual songs, 27, 72, 73
spiritual warfare, 92
stature, 87
strength, 18, 35, 42, 45, 48, 87, 97, 103
stripes, 58, 78
stronghold, 62
strongholds, 14
success, 76, 94

sweet aroma, 105
swine, 9
sword, 24
system, 58, 66, 77

T

tabernacle, 5
talents, 70
Talibans, 86
tax collectors, 108
tears, 5, 6, 25, 33
temperance, 63, 97
temple, 29, 71, 99
temptation, 36
territory, 48
thanksgiving, 21, 28, 46, 57, 74
Thomas, 25
thousand, 3, 50, 76, 103
throne, 5, 35
tolerance, 108
tongue, 7, 29, 60
tower, 19
traffic, 24
transgressions, 10
trespasses, 40, 43
tribes, 94
triumph, 73
trumpet, 6
trust, 2, 25, 48
truth, 10, 31, 39, 51, 52, 74, 80, 91, 107, 108

U

unbelief, 25
uncleanness, 64
understanding, 14, 57
universe, 101
unrighteousness, 10, 64

V

vainglory, 31
vengeance, 17
victory, 4, 82, 100
violator, 69
visitations, 54
vocabulary, 24
voice, 5, 35, 53, 60, 95, 101
voiceless, 56
vows, 15

W

wars, 26
waters, 39, 53
weakness, 41
weapons, 3
weight, 77
wife, 15, 23, 109
will of God, 13, 88

wine, 27, 73
wisdom, 10, 13, 41, 82, 87, 88, 103, 104, 107, 108
Wisdom of Solomon, 103
wise, 8, 15, 41, 81, 87
witchcraft, 56
witnesses, 81
Word of God, 90
worship, 92, 102
wrath, 17
wrong, 11, 17, 88

Y

yoke, 20
youth, 108

Z

Zambia, 86, 94
Zion, 91